HOW TO WRITE A ROMANCE NOVEL

I would highly recommend and strongly encourage that all writers who are seriously considering to pursue their writing careers, take advantage of Susan's enthusiam and professional skills that she so willingly shares with her students.

I honestly believe her teaching techniques and methods will prove helpful for writers at all skill levels.

Susan is not only a great teacher, but helped to influence me to continue with my own writing goals. I myself look forward to more of Susan's upcoming classes in the near future.
Patty Koontz, author

I have been a student in Susan's synopsis class and she is a wonderful teacher. Her lessons are easy to follow and get results. She has taught me so much and I received a contract after working with her. If you follow her advice, you too will get amazing results.
Susan Jaymes, author of *Guilty Hearts*, Desert Breeze Publishing

I'm pleased to endorse Susan Palmquist's forthcoming book. I recently had the pleasure of editing two of her fiction books written under the pen name Vanessa Devereaux.

Ms. Palmquist is a talented and knowledgeable writer with an innate sense of story. I've worked with many romance authors over the years, and Ms. Palmquist impressed me with her flair for language, her ability to get inside her characters' heads and hearts, and her consummate professionalism. I have the utmost confidence in her knowledge and experience as a romance author.
Lynne Anderson, Editor and former editor, Cobblestone Press

How to Write a Romance Novel

A Beginner's Guide to Getting
it Written and Getting it Published

How to Write a Romance Novel

A Beginner's Guide to Getting it Written and Getting it Published

Susan Palmquist

COMPASS BOOKS

Winchester, UK
Washington, USA

First published by Compass Books, 2012
Compass Books is an imprint of John Hunt Publishing Ltd., Laurel House, Station Approach,
Alresford, Hants, SO24 9JH, UK
office1@jhpbooks.net
www.johnhuntpublishing.com
www.compass-books.net

For distributor details and how to order please visit the 'Ordering' section on our website.

Text copyright: Susan Palmquist 2012

ISBN: 978 1 78099 467 3

A CIP catalogue record for this book is available from the British Library.

Design: Stuart Davies

Printed and bound by CPI Group (UK) Ltd, Croydon, CR0 4YY

We operate a distinctive and ethical publishing philosophy in all
areas of our business, from our global network of authors to
production and worldwide distribution.

CONTENTS

Dedication

For Jeff, and to my parents for always believing in me as a writer even when the rejection letters piled up. And last but not least, to all my writing students both past and present.

Introduction

Let me start this book with a confession-

I never intended to become a romance writer.

I'd grown up reading every mystery novel I could get my hands on. I was obsessed with anything written by Agatha Christie, and lived vicariously through Enid Blyton's Secret Seven. When I decided I wanted to be a writer my heart was set on becoming a crime novelist.

When one rejection led to another I realized things weren't looking that great about me attaining that goal. But then a fellow writer suggested I give romance writing a try. Problem was I didn't know much about that genre. Besides sneaking a peek at the Mills and Boon romances my maternal grandmother always brought along in her suitcase during visits with us, that was about the sum of my knowledge.

This fellow writer, who I should say was already published, gave me a vital insider's secret. Romance sells better than any other genre, and is a great way to get on the first step of the ladder to becoming a multi-published author.

So off I headed to the library and bookstores and immersed myself in the world of Harlequin, Silhouette and Bantam's Loveswept novels.

My goal was to know everything there was about romances and what made them so popular. The idea was to start writing and selling my stories to publishers, and then once I'd made a name for myself, I get back to what I really wanted to do, craft bestselling mysteries.

Reading all these books was good training for me but I have to admit that my first attempts at penning a romance were complete failures. One very famous editor in the business whose name I won't mention even attached a handwritten note on one rejection slip telling me to think about doing something else because I'd never be a writer.

Luckily I didn't believe her and kept trying. As I put more energy into it I learned about both writing romances, and writing in general. I'll skip forward in this story because I took an unintentional ten years off from writing after my father died. By the time I decided to pull out some old manuscripts and start sending them out again, the whole publishing world had changed.

Publishers had merged which meant fewer markets. And fewer publishers would accept manuscripts from un-agented writers. However, electronic books were starting to gain popularity and once again it looked like romances were the hot commodity in that format too. It was now or never, and I'm happy to say I did finally get my romance published. My first book A Sterling Affair was published in both electronic and print, and a second one, Sleeping With Fairies followed shortly after. And yes, I did finally get a mystery (Death Likes Me) published but I'll make another confession. I would never give up writing romances because they're fun and exciting stories to create.

Since my first successes, I now also write under a pen name, Vanessa Devereaux, and yes did become a bestselling author on Barnes and Noble's Fictionwise book and All Romance E Books sites.

Besides my writing, I also share my knowledge and yes, many of mistakes along the way to publication, with students in workshops, and one on one as a tutor for a UK-based writing school.

I decided to write this book not only to share what I've learned on my journey but I hope that my story will serve as an inspiration to you as you put pen to paper, or fingers to the keyboard. My advice is to practice your craft, look at each day as a learning experience to become a better writer than you were the day before. And most of all; never, never give up on your dreams.

Reasons to Write A Romance

You might already be a fan of romance novels and one day decided you wanted to write your own. This is a perfect background for doing just that because you already have some *insider* information about the genre. However, here are a couple of other reasons romance novels are perfect for the beginning writer-

The huge and continually growing market means that publishers are constantly looking for new writers. If you've ever checked out publisher's Web sites or writer's directories like Writer's Digest, you'll often see the dreaded words *agented submissions only* next to many of the big name companies. If you don't have an agent you're out of luck getting your manuscript into the hands of an editor who might very well love your story. However, one exception is they'll often look at a romance manuscript. You can get your foot in the door whereas a mystery or sci-fi writer might need to find an agent to submit to the very same publishing house.

Another reason is the ever growing electronic market. Once again romance novels have taken off the fastest in this format. A new electronic publisher seems to open their doors for business every week which is great news for the beginning writer. Not that I'm saying it's any easier to get published because you still need to write a great story, but at least your work is read and evaluated on an equal footing with published authors.

What You'll Find in this Book

My goal in writing this book is to not only give you the tools that you'll need to write and sell a romance novel but I'm hoping it will become your ultimate guide to writing one. When I sat down to write this my aim was to make it the one and only book you'll ever need on the topic. For that reason I decided to approach it differently to other books I've read about romance writing.

I've created chapters on key elements that I feel are essential to a crafting a successful romance novel. Things like conflict, emotion, and sexual tension that are usually grouped together in various chapters in other books. I've decided to give them their own turn in this book and for that reason you might find some chapters shorter than others but nevertheless equally important. I also hope that by doing so it helps you use this book a reference you'll turn to even when you're published. I'd like to think that you'll use it as quick guide when you work on your edits.

While I'll cover key aspects such as characterization, dialogue, and point of view that can be applied to any type of story, each chapter focuses specifically on the romance genre. At the end of each chapter you'll find some exercises for you to try, and key points of that chapter.

If you've only been thinking about writing or working on the manuscript I hope this book will help you get started, polish the story and yes, sell it too.

Okay, let's get started...

Chapter One

What is a Romance Novel?

Types of Romance Novels

Ask an editor or writer what exactly is a romance novel and I'll bet you'll never get the same response from any two people. And that's because the romance genre offers a wide array of stories for just about everyone's taste.

From the traditional Mills and Boon and Harlequin romances to family sagas that span generations and centuries, and then to chick lit. Romance novels have and remain firm favorites with readers.

It's not just a love story, but a journey a couple takes from the first meeting to the rocky start, the complications along the way, and then to the eventual happy ever after.

The major sub genres of romance stories include-

Traditional Romance

Romance Suspense

Medical Romances

Historical Romances

Erotic Romances

Steam punk Romance

Inspirational Romance

Gothic Romance

Regency Romance

Paranormal Romance

More about all these sub genres later in the book.

Places You Can Sell Romances

I've already mentioned print and electronic publishers but the market doesn't stop there. There are audio book markets, pocket novels such as those published by DC Thomson (The People's Friend and My Weekly) in the UK. And if you read magazines, you already know that romances or boy-meets-girl types of stories are perennial favorites in the short story genre too.

A Promising Future

Just like the stories themselves, the romance genre has a promising outlook. Even during economic downturns, readers love romances better than any other genres so it's almost like entering a recession-proof business.

Finding Ideas for Romance Stories

Ask any writer what's the most common question they're asked and I'll guess that *where do you get your ideas?* tops their list. So if you're wondering where you'll get your inspiration for all these wonderful stories that are waiting to be told, here are some ideas to get you started.

The Story and Idea Book

When I began writing I used to get ideas for stories pop into my head but by the time I sat down to write, I'd forgotten all about them or at least the crucial parts. Something I learned to do early on was to use a story and idea book. It doesn't have to be fancy, just a plain notebook will do, but keep it close to you at all times. If I have a dentist's appointment, I've been known to throw mine into my purse just in case the muse strikes while I'm in the waiting room. And don't forget to write down *everything*. Even if it's doesn't make sense right at that minute or it's just something like a brilliant piece of dialogue that springs into your mind. Sometimes when I'm about to start a new story I'll look through the notebook and see what jumps out at me. It might be a story outline, notes about a certain character that's been swirling around in my head, or even a place I've visited that I think will make a great setting for a romance. Creating your own book assures you that you'll never run out of ideas or forget what could the next bestseller.

Looking To Real Life

If ideas don't come to you…and be assured they eventually will, sometimes all you need to do is read a magazine or newspaper or even turn on the news. Some of my stories have come via articles I've stumbled across. It could be someone with an unusual profession that's so unique it's not been done before and therefore will be fresh to editors and readers. It might be an article about couples who met through strange circumstances… another way to give your story a different twist.

Sometimes I make notes of these but most of the time I cut them out, fold them up and tape them inside my story and idea book. And hang on to them even if you don't use them straightaway. I have a couple of newspaper articles in my book that, yes, I'll admit it, they are browning around the edges but I know I'll use them one of these days.

What Do you Want to write?

Okay, with idea in hand, it's time to start narrowing down what type of book you want to write. My first piece of advice is to think about what type of stories you enjoy reading. The reason being, you've probably read more in this sub genre and therefore know some of the 'givens' of those types of stories. For example, I love romantic suspense so I know what I look when I pick one up and hence what an editor will want to see in my manuscript.

Do you like historical settings? Or are you a fan of the traditional Harlequin romance where love scenes are far and few between, if at all. Or do you like steamy romances like Harlequin Blaze that are more like true life?

One thing I tell my students not to do is write in a genre or sub genre that they don't like but instead force themselves to do it just because it's the *in* thing right now. You might strike gold but sometimes forcing yourself to write a story you don't enjoy can hurt your chances of selling a manuscript. And reality says by the time your story is accepted and published, that hot trend is probably cooling off. Another word of warning; erotic romances are popular now, especially in the electronic market, but if you're not comfortable about writing scenes using frank language and describing explicit sexual situations, your uneasiness is going to come across in your manuscript too.

If at this point you're not sure what appeals to you, read as many romance novels as you can and narrow it down. I know from experience this task can get expensive so go to your local library and pick a couple of historical, family saga, suspense etc.

Another tip I give to my students, and this not only helps you with selecting what type of book you'd like to write, but with your overall writing too is to become a reviewer. Check the resource guide at the back of the book for some sites that are always looking for reviewers. It's also the perfect way to see who's publishing what type of stories so you'll know who to target when it's time to submit your manuscript.

Key Points

Romance is and always has been the most popular of the genres.

Many publishers who won't accept non-agented submissions will look at romance stories.

Pick a sub genre that you enjoy reading the most.

Think about being a reviewer to get an idea of what's being published and by whom.

Something for You to Try

Read at least one book from the major romance sub genres. What did you like most about it? What did you like the least? Based on your research, have you decided what type of story you want to write?

Chapter Two

Characterization

This chapter focuses on one of the key elements of a romance and that's the people whose story you'll tell and whose point of view the reader will experience the ups and down of your tale.

What Makes a Good Character?

Think about a book you enjoyed reading…one that was almost impossible to put down until you'd finished the last word (It doesn't have to be a romance, any genre will do).

How many of you think the plot held your interest? And how many think it was one or more of the characters that had you spellbound?

Without me actually knowing your responses I know I'd be safe in saying that the higher percentage would go to characters and not plot.

There's no question about it that a good, strong plot is vital to any book. However, unless you create at least one character that your reader can identify with, having the most fantastic plot in the world won't have as much impact.

A memorable and stand-out character beckons the reader and says come along with me because I have this story to tell you. It's that larger than life person whose eyes and head you experience the joy, the sorrow, the laughter, and sometimes the pain, in the book.

A great character is someone that the reader can relate to, sympathize with, cheer for, cry with, and yes, remember long after you've finished reading the story. So how does a writer create that memorable character every time they sit down to pen a story?

Make Them Identifiable

Start thinking about the book that lived on in your memory. What was it that you liked about the character so much? I think for most readers, myself included, it's because I could indentify with them.

My formal education is in psychology and counseling and one of the first things we were taught is that most clients will come along looking for help with a problem they think only they have, or a fear only they're experiencing. However, ninety-nine percent of the time they're wrong. The truth is most of us are more alike than we are different.

We all have fears and while they might not be the exact same ones for each of us, there's something out there in the world that makes us feel uneasy. It could be a dread about public speaking. Maybe it's a fear of spiders or the fear of being left all alone without family and friends when we get old. The same goes for the characters you create. Make them like the people who will be reading their story and you've formed an immediate bond.

As most of us haven't all read the same books but are probably more familiar with TV shows, many of the examples I'll give you in this book are from the screen and not the page.

One example I'll offer here which I think illustrates this point is the TV show *Lost*. If you watched it you'll remember that every week we had a flashback to a different character's life before they crashed on the island. We got to see the character develop twice. And in my opinion one of the reasons this show was a huge success.

I think it worked perfectly because you got to see who they were and why they sometimes acted like they did on the island. Kate and Sawyer hadn't been model citizens. Sawyer was a con man and Kate was on the run for killing her step-father. However, you got to know them as people, saw their side of the story through their point of view, and in fact, came to like them so much that you hated when bad things happened to them (like getting kidnapped by The Others). And why were The Others so hated by us, yep, we didn't already *know* them and hadn't invested an interest in these people.

In the third season, two characters appeared in the show who supposedly were crash survivors but up till then we'd never seen them and didn't know their back story. When it came time for their flashback about them poisoning a guy and stealing his diamonds, you couldn't sympathize with them because you felt like you didn't know and understand why they'd done this bad thing. In fact, you were happy both of them died during that episode.

Case in point, let your readers know all about your characters, Why they're the people that they are and do it through great point of view. When they know exactly what the characters are feeling they'll love them all (even the bad guys).

Maybe you're writing a romantic suspense novel and the bad guys are chasing your character with guns drawn and about to shoot them. Hopefully, none of us will ever find ourselves in such a predicament but we can imagine what they're experiencing. We know these people are wondering am I going to make it out of this situation alive? Who's going to take care of my children if I die? I didn't get to tell my parents that I love them. You can imagine their heart is beating double time and maybe perspiration is breaking out on their forehead. I think you can easily see how you'd relate to this character even if they're in a situation you've never found yourself in, and how you'd be cheering for them to escape.

The same goes for other emotions besides fear. Envy, happiness, and in the case of romance; falling in love. Whether we're eighteen or eighty, we all know what it's like to spot their special someone across the room. To meet that person who we fall in love with and who changes our lives forever.

And I'll round up my examples with one of my own characters Niki Webber from **Death Likes Me.** I knew I wanted to write a series so I had to give her some issues to deal with. And yes, did I give her lots of things to try and cope with. She's only thirty-eight but already a widow. She's been shot in the line of duty and almost died. Oh, and for good measure I threw in that she's guilt-ridden because she thinks she might have wanted to end her life and hence the reason she let her guard down and got shot. And because of that her partner had to shoot a teenage boy who hadn't been in any trouble before.

You might be thinking well, not everyone's been shot in the line of duty and caused the death of a young boy, but guilt is a universal feeling and losing a spouse is something many people have or will face.

Give Them A Past

Most great characters have something in their past that's not only shaped who they are but also a weight they carry with them in the present day. It also dictates their future behavior too. It might even be one of those little quirks readers love so much.

Two examples that fit into the above category are the TV shows Monk and House.

Here's why I've picked them to illustrate my point. Adrian Monk whose wife was killed by a car bomb is not only on a quest to find her killer, but he's trying to get back on the police force. And while trying to achieve those two goals, he's got a phobia about many things most of us wouldn't bat an eye at and yes, it hinders not only his every day activities but his two main goals.

So why can we identify with him if he's such an odd character? We can feel his loss about his wife's senseless murder and his need to find the person responsible. We can also understand why he wants to return to a job he once loved.

Example number two is Gregory House, MD. He walks with a cane, is addicted to painkillers, and despite being a brilliant doctor who many have said is really Sherlock Holmes in the medical field; the man's a complete pain in the butt to not only his fellow doctors but patients too. So why can so many people identity with this is this rude and obnoxious character and be held under his spell? We've all been in pain and some of us have had something happen that's changed not only the way we physically cope with life but changed our outlook on it too.

And here's an example of one of my works in progress. It's early in the story and I've used this scene as the first one in the hero's point of view. He's hiding something but the heroine doesn't know exactly what and I've used it to give the reader some insight into his character-

How was he going to get himself out of this one? He hadn't planned on getting hit by a car. If that wasn't bad enough, the car's driver was the ultimate Good Samaritan.

Sophie handed the pharmacist her credit card for his painkillers. She'd insisted she pay for them. Maybe her being so generous wasn't such a bad thing because at this very moment he had a grand total of $2.45 in his pocket.

He glanced over at the pharmacy window again. She was slipping the credit card back into her bag. He barely knew this woman, but he'd already taken a liking to her. Correct that, he'd been blown away by her cute face and curvy body when he'd seen her standing by her car looking down at him.

He eyed her from the top of her golden blonde hair right down to her shapely ankles. He had more important things on his mind but it didn't hurt to take a few minutes to admire the great view while he could. And what a pity he hadn't met her under better circumstances.

She turned around as if she sensed he was watching her. She smiled at him. He smiled back. The pharmacist handed her a white paper bag. Hopefully, its contents would take the edge off the sharp pain in his side which right now felt like a hot knife ripping through his skin. However, his first concern was getting rid of Sophie. Not that he really wanted to, but he had to for her own safety.

She walked over to him.

"Don't take the pills on an empty stomach and don't drink any alcohol while you're taking them." She handed him the bag.

His stomach chose that particular moment to rumble several times. It must have heard her mention the word *empty*.

He hadn't eaten in over twenty-four hours. What type of meal could you buy for just $2.45? Didn't Arby's and McDonalds advertise dollar menu meals? He couldn't risk using his credit cards or drawing money from his account. Maybe he should find the nearest fast food restaurant to see what his meager money could buy.

"I'll drop you off at your hotel," said Sophie.

"Are you sure I'm not stopping you from doing anything else? Something more important than playing chauffeur to me?"

"No, I'd planned to take the afternoon off after the doctor's visit so I'd only be heading home had I not ..."

"Run into me."

He tried to walk at a normal pace to the car, but the hot knives were still clawing at him. And the tape was beginning to pull on his chest hair. Could things get any worse for him?

"So where to?" Sophie slipped the key into the ignition.

He had to think quickly and hoped he didn't make a slip she'd pick up on.

"The Economy Suites."

She frowned at him. Yep, he'd made a slip.

"We don't have Economy Suites here in Portland?"

"Did I say Economy Suites? That's where I was staying last week. I meant the Days Inn." He hoped he'd said the right thing this time.

"So where are you from?"

Although pretty, she asked too many questions.

"Idaho." That was the first state that had popped into his head. He hoped she didn't ask him more questions like where in Idaho he lived or what he did for a living.

He hated lying.

He was in luck because she pulled into the parking lot of a hotel. By pure chance, he'd obviously picked the closest one to the Medical Arts Building. He was safe now. He could exit the car and not have to answer any more questions. If he stayed in her presence any longer, pretty soon he was going to lie himself into a circle he couldn't escape from. He sensed she was already curious about his shabby appearance and the slip up about the hotel.

"Do you need any help getting to your room?"

"No, I'll be fine. You've been a great help to me. Thank you." He held out his hand to her.

She shook it.

"Goodbye." He opened the car door.

"Goodbye and good luck. I hope the bruises heal soon."

He shut the door, turned and walked toward the hotel entrance. Mike glanced back at her one last time. She waved before driving away.

He held his side and took a deep breath when a sharp pain shot through his ribs. He wouldn't have time to find someplace to get a cheap snack. Right now he needed to get the painkillers inside him ASAP.

Mike entered the first restroom he'd spotted when he'd walked into the lobby. He took out the bottle of pills, popped off the top and shook a tablet out into his palm. Tossing one into his mouth, he leaned over the sink, turned on the taps and swallowed the water until the pill was safely down his throat.

He raised his head to look in the mirror.

Shit, what a mess.

Mike ran his hands under the tap before dragging them through his hair. He couldn't remember the last time he'd brushed his teeth, taken a shower or any of the other mundane day-to-day activities he'd once taken for granted.

Leaning over the sink again, he splashed his face, hoping that would help his appearance. Glancing in the mirror, he realized it hadn't helped a whole lot, but at least it had refreshed him.

He couldn't stay in the restroom forever. It was time to consider his next move. Where would he spend the night? If he could get some rest, hide out somewhere for awhile, he'd be able to think about what to do next.

Mike exited the restroom and headed into the lobby but stopped in his tracks. Sophie hadn't driven away like he'd thought. She was sitting in a chair in the reception area with her legs crossed, dangling one of her shiny black pumps from her right foot.

Should he just dive back into the restroom before she saw him? That would be a wise move, but right now he couldn't move. The sight of Sophie sitting there, those gorgeous legs on full display had him totally mesmerized and his feet felt like they were glued to the floor.

She looked over at him. He'd been caught red handed. He'd have to play this cool, like he was surprised to see her again, and not to mention so soon after saying goodbye.

He strolled over to her, offering her his best smile. That usually got him out of trouble with women. Well, at least it did when his teeth were brushed, his hair combed and his face shaven. Now he might not be so appealing.

"Did you forget something?" Or maybe I forgot something," he said.

"I think it's you who did the forgetting. Like forgetting you're not staying at this hotel. Or maybe you sustained amnesia when my car hit you?"

Yep, he'd been right about her. She was not only beautiful but smart too.

Secondary Characters

No chapter on characterization would be complete without a mention of secondary characters. Some of the shorter category romance books won't offer you much room for adding supporting players but if you're thinking about writing the longer or more mainstream romances, secondary characters can add a whole new level to the story. Here are a few reasons why I think they work and what they can do-

They Move the Plot

One of the rules of top notch writing is to move the plot with every sentence. Adding a colorful secondary character allows you do just that. It might be a conversation between the hero and heroine and the secondary character. Or it could be a scene where the secondary character tells someone about the main character and what happened to them.

They Can Add a Touch of Suspense or Even Evil

The main characters can't be all bad or all good because they won't come across as real, therefore adding a villain into the mix justifies their actions. The main character might be in pursuit of the villain and they might be tested by the character. They could even be forced to save the heroine by taking the villain's life. The main character is able to show their true colors by interacting with the villain and best of all, it's believable.

They Take the Story Up a Notch

Sometimes a character can be a perfect sparring partner for one of your main characters. They might get under their skin so you'll able to reveal something else about their personality when they react to this person. Do they get angry, remain calm, or what?

They Can Give You a Ready Made Sub Plot

If you're writing a longer novel, you will need a sub plot. What better way to ease that into your story than with another character and a mini story that interacts with the main story line.

They're Just Plain Fun

Even if you're not writing a romantic comedy, a secondary character can add some humor and more depth to your story and break up the tension a bit for the reader

Character Sketches

So how do you make sure you've created someone who fits in with all of the above? For me it means letting them live in my head for a few weeks, even months before I start putting them on the computer screen. I think of them as real people and how they would react in certain situations. However, if you're a person who likes to write everything down before you get started, one good aid is a character outline. The great thing is once you've have this stored on your computer or notebook you can use it time and again.

Here's one that I've used for many years. Another plus to creating it is it also helps you keep track of names, and whose who, which can all too easily get confused when you start composing-

Character's Name
Nickname
Place of Birth
Where they live now
Occupation
Family
Parents still alive, yes or no
Happy childhood yes or no, if no, what happened?
Social and political beliefs
Hobbies
Involved in any groups? If so which ones?
Illnesses or accidents that impact their personality
Schooling, what did they study?
Past relationships, have they been engaged or married before?

Any children?

How do they feel about getting involved in a relationship at this point in their lives?

You can add or take away anything from the above outline sketch. And as you work on your second, third or fourth story you might want to tweak it even more.

When you're creating this character sketch you might be surprised how something will jump out at you and you think, great I can use that as a sub plot or conflict.

Problems for characters

One thing that all books must have is conflict. Writing doesn't have any real rules but I think like to think the following is a must, no conflict, no story, no story...no sale.

Lack of conflict is one of the major reasons manuscripts get rejected. Create well-rounded characters with problems that aren't easily solved and you've got conflict. Pair them against someone else with their own problem and an opposing conflict, and you've got trouble. And yes, the makings of a great story.

Key Points

Characters can make or break a story.

Even if you have a great plot, sometimes a manuscript is rejected because the reader...in this case an editor, didn't connect to the character.

Make your main characters people who the reader can identify with.

Create your own character sketch that you can use for your current and future stories.

Something For You To Try

Think about a book you've enjoyed reading. Maybe it's one of the keepers on your shelf. Now think about the characters in that book. What did you like about them? How had the writer portrayed them? How did the author get you to identify and maybe sympathize with them?

Chapter Three

Dialogue

In this chapter you'll learn about what makes for good dialogue in a story and how to put the perfect words into your character's mouths. In the previous chapter I said writing doesn't have any real rules, here's another tiny exception that I've always stuck to (because I've heard it said by most editors), and that's a book should be around sixty percent dialogue. Knowing that you can see how a lot rests on getting it just right.

Dialogue Can Make Or Break a Story

Do you after find yourself remembering certain words from movies? Some people still quote lines from films that hit the screens fifty or sixty years ago. You might think they're recalling some actor's snappy one liner or come back to another player, when in fact you're remembering a screenwriter's great gift for penning compelling dialogue.

What Dialogue Does For Your Story

Ever given up reading a novel because you didn't like it but didn't quite know why? Was the pacing slow or the characters flat? Maybe the dialogue didn't sound real enough? For me, what separates an okay book from a great one is oftentimes natural sounding dialogue. Dialogue has many roles to play in a story. I think of it as the story's workhorse because it carries a lot of weight and can achieve so much. Great dialogue has the following characteristics-

Natural Sounding.

It doesn't sound too formal, has contradictions, and some slang thrown in there. Forget about the spell and grammar checker feature on your computer. When it says you've created a fragment and it's highlighting a piece of your dialogue, it means you've hit the jackpot. You've more than likely created natural sounding speech.

It Doesn't Try and Tell the Whole Story in One or Two Character's Lines

Some writers yes, even published ones, use dialogue as a vehicle to tell the reader everything they want them to know about another character or even the plot. I don't care if you're writing your first or 100th book, it never works and most of the time angers your reader. Take it slow, don't put words into your character's mouths all at once…feed it to them slowly.

Doesn't Tell the Other Characters Information they Already Know Just for the Sole Purpose of Telling the Reader.

Right now you're probably saying what is she talking about? The easiest way to explain this minor sin is to give you an example. And yes, some of you who are fans of these shows will hate me but I think it's so perfect that I can't think of a better way to get the point across.

It's the CSI shows, and I'm sorry to say one of the reasons I'm not a fan. Every time I've watched one of them there's always been a scene between two characters who are both supposedly forensic experts. One however is explaining to the other one what they're doing. *I'm putting this under the microscope to look for latent fingerprints.* Sure I don't know that because I don't work in that field but if you were working with someone who did, why would you need to spell it out to them? If a co-worker did that to you wouldn't you think, *duh, why are you telling me that? Someone drop you on your head this morning or what?* I know the goal is to tell us information and tell it in a speedy manner but it might work for a TV show that only has about forty minutes to convey the story, but it doesn't work for novels and comes across as lazy writing, yet authors do it all the time.

It's Distinctive to the Character

Done right it allows the reader to know just who's doing the talking. It's specific to each of your characters. It might be the way the character phrases something or even pauses between words or thoughts. Dialogue is a great way to make your character memorable too. Wouldn't books be boring if all the characters sounded exactly alike? Unfortunately, that's the reason many manuscript get rejected. When a writer uses top notch dialogue you know who's speaking.

It Reveals Character

Remember the last chapter about how to create memorable characters? Through their dialogue you can tell your reader a lot about each one without you having to actually tell them a thing. Through dialogue a reader can learn that a character maybe has an accent, or that English isn't their first language. It might even tell you exactly where they're from. Depending on the contractions and slang you use or don't use, can also reveal the social class of your character. And dialogue can even reveal time. For example, the way people spoke during the Regency is different to the way we talk in modern times. Maybe the character swears, maybe they have a unique way of saying something, or maybe it's the way they string their words together.

It Reveals and Progresses the Plot

When you think about dialogue, revealing plot doesn't automatically jump out at you but you can tell the reader about what's already happened, what's happening, and what's about to happen through dialogue. One character revealing something the reader hasn't known up till that point in the story. Maybe they've always been in love with the other character, or that they don't want to be in relationship with them. It's a great vehicle for you the writer to get out of the picture and let your character *tell* the story.

Something most of us don't think about when we put the words into our character's mouths is that their dialogue can actually help move the story forward. Readers don't want all narration in the same way they don't want all dialogue so it's the perfect way to mix things up in a story.

It Can Up the Suspense

I'm not talking about suspense like in a crime novel; although dialogue can definitely work there too. Suspense in a romance novel could be that the hero reveals to the heroine that he's really on the run from the law.

Here is another example from my book **Death Likes Me** that I hope will show you how you can achieve some of what I've just told about dialogue. It's a scene between the main character Niki Webber and another character who she believes is hiding something from her-

I followed behind him when he left the classroom that day.

"I'm going to my office. You do know where that is, don't you?"

I followed him there and he shut the door.

"Why did you break in here?"

"You just invited me in."

"Shit, don't be so smug."

"The matchbook, where did you get it?"

"First of all, you're interested in my sex life, now it's my purchasing habits."

"The matchbook, where?"

"I picked them up from a café. I do it all the time. I didn't know it was a crime."

"You know where they're from?"

"Jesus Christ, just get to the point."

"They're from the Chisholm fish processing plant in Cove Bay."

"So?"

"I've mentioned the Chisholms before. Do you know the family, Paul Chisholm in particular?"

He took out a packet of cigarettes from his jacket pocket and then threw it on the chair once he'd realized it was empty.

"No, should I?"

"Chloe worked for them. She left their house about two weeks before she died. If you didn't see Chloe, how do you explain a matchbook from their head office in Cove Bay?"

"I've never been there, so someone probably gave me that matchbook. We borrow them all the time around here."

"What would you say if I told you I don't believe one word of that bullshit?"

"Then I'd say that's your problem, not mine."

"Seems a bit of coincidence, doesn't it? Chloe works for a family that live miles out of town and you just happen to end up with the matchbook from the family's company. And how about sleeping pills? Chloe's system had traces of some type of sleeping drug. Had any reason to take any lately?"

He didn't answer.

"I'm going to call the police."

He picked up the receiver.

I stood, ready to leave.

"Go ahead. Don't let me stop you."

I left and closed the door. He was going to call someone, just not the police. I put my ear close to the door.

"Babe, we've got big trouble."

It Can Speed Up the Pacing

Nothing earns a writer a rejection letter faster than slow pacing. One way you can speed it up is with dialogue rather then pages upon pages of narration where *you* tell the reader the story instead of your characters.

It Moves the Story Forward

Also related to the pacing is dialogue can move the story forward to a new scene or even to a new time.

It Can Ease Conflict and Put the Reader at Ease

I've already mentioned how dialogue can spring some surprises on the reader by what a character reveals, and it can do the reverse too. After a tense scene, say a fight between the hero and heroine, you can put the reader at ease by having one character telling the other one he didn't really mean the words he said.

Creating Top Notch Dialogue Each Time

One thing I've been told by most of my editors is that dialogue is my greatest strength as a writer. I'll admit sometimes once I get started on a scene with dialogue I forsake description and my editors have to get me back on track. However, it has given me lots of practice and here I'd like to share with you some of the techniques I've been using-

Practice

I've found that rather then avoid things you're not good at, practice can make perfect. So how about spending ten or twenty minutes a day just writing some dialogue? Select two of your own characters or take two from a book you're reading and start up a conversation between them. See if you can incorporate all of the essential qualities I've listed. You won't be able to do it every time but try to cover at least half of them. While writing it, what do you find the hardest? Is this something you need to work on some more?

Become an Eavesdropper to Make it Sound Realistic

When you're a writer you've got the perfect excuse to be an eavesdropper. Listening in to other's conversations not only garners ideas for future stories, but it lets you hear how real people talk. Remember it's these *real* people you want to put into your stories. I love to sit in a waiting room, restaurant, and on public transportation and listen in to other people's conversations. I especially listen to the way they way they pause and the way some people finish other's sentences for them. And how about the person who dominates a conversation? Close your eyes and listen to how people around you speak. What types of words do they use? Are there words and terms you've never heard before?

Read Dialogue

One way to learn great dialogue is to read a screenplay. For a screenwriter dialogue has to be their biggest asset or they don't make a living, and for that reason they've become the kings of the art. (In the resource section of the book I've listed where you can order screenplays to read).

Read Aloud

One thing I do when I'm editing my work be it fiction or non-fiction is to read it aloud. You'll hear what's working and what's not, and this is especially true for dialogue.

What Not To Do With Dialogue

Now I've told you how to fine tune your dialogue writing skills, here are a few things you should never try to accomplish using only dialogue.

Don't Give Us an Information Dump

One easy way to get a rejection or for the reader to close your book and not pick it up again is the dreaded information dump.

One character telling the other everything that's happened so far so we, the reader, can get caught up too.

He Said, He Shouted, She Screamed

I bring up this side topic because one thing you don't want the editor to know about you is that you're a new writer. One way to do that is to use tags like he shouted, she screamed throughout your whole manuscript. One or two might be okay but instead stick with just said and use your showing skills to let the reader know the character raised their voice or got angry as the words spilled out of their mouths. Have him bang the table so hard the plates jump up in the air.

Accents

One question that I'm always asked in the workshops I teach is should you write in accents. My response is you can but just don't overdo it. You might know what it's supposed to sound like but unless you're an expert on accents, you can leave the reader confused more than enlightened. As a beginning writer I'd say, use it but with caution because you don't want to put the editor off your manuscript by making him or her have to read the same sentence or passage a couple of times trying to figure out what your characters are trying to say.

Key Points

Dialogue is the workhorse of writing because it can achieve so much.

To develop a realistic ear for dialogue, listen to the way real people talk and communicate.

Don't be afraid to use bad grammar or sentence fragments when you're using dialogue because it can allow the reader to get to know one character from another.

Read screenplays to get a feel for top notch dialogue.

Something for you to try

What book are you reading right now? Search through it and find a section with lots of dialogue.

What did you learn from it? Anything about the plot or anything about the characters?

How did it advance the plot?

What did it reveal about the character who was talking?

What if you didn't like it?

What was wrong with it?

Rewrite it yourself and see if you can improve it.

Chapter Four

Point of View

In this chapter you'll learn all about Point of View (POV) and how it pulls together everything from character to plot in a story.

What is POV?

You won't find two definitions of POV remotely the same but here's mine. It's how the reader enters and then experiences your story. When we pick up a book it's whose eyes, head, thoughts and emotions we live that story through. It's the person who says come along with me because I've got this story to tell you. As writers our toughest job is getting our readers to *see* everything that's in our heads (through the character's perception), feel everything we're putting these characters through, and when we do all that successfully it's due to proper and correct POV.

Why POV is Vital

Whether you're writing a 1,000 word story or one with 100,000 words, POV is the lifeblood of that story and here's why-

POV is Inter-connected with Other Elements of the Storytelling Process. For example, Voice, Character and Plot.

It's almost like the backbone of the story into which all these elements are built and refined.

POV Can Turn a Ho-Hum Story, and Even a Hackneyed Plot, into a Great Read.

I've told you that romance is a huge genre and its one drawback is that editors see many of the same storylines over and over again. One way to give them something fresh and increase your chances of making a sale, is to tweak a plot, and one easy way to do that is by changing POV.

POV Can Affect the Reader's Experience

Not handling POV properly can make the story jarring for someone to read. Another problem is using the wrong one, or even head-hopping, can ruin an otherwise great story.

POV Can Make a Story More Emotional.

All readers love something that tugs at their emotions but it's especially vital to the romance.

POV Can Give You a Unique Writer's Voice

One thing you don't want is for your stories to sound like everybody else's. Tweaking POV can give you the unique voice. In fact, it can refine your writer's voice.

Types of POV

We've all sat through, (yes, suffered too,) grammar at school so you probably remember the teacher telling you all about tenses. I won't bore you again but tenses are related to POV so I'll touch upon them, but I promise you it's going to be brief.

Present. She is walking to the window.

Past. She walked to the window.

Future. She will walk to the window.

It's basically the way your story is told to the reader and using a different tense can sometimes alter POV and give your story a unique twist.

Who's on First?

Another thing you probably remember from grammar is the whole first, second, and third person elements. It's also interconnected with POV so I'll touch upon that briefly here too.

First

First person narration-I walked to the window.

Many books, including mysteries are told via first person, and also some of the old gothic romances too.

Second person narration-You walked to the window

Not the most common way to tell a story but it has been done.

Third Person Narration-She walked to the window.

Third person is the most common and probably what most writers are comfortable using.

And Finally…

There's also omniscient. **John Smith sensed that something out there in the universe would cause him to walk to the window.** I call it the all knowing narration and it's mostly found in the big blockbuster books of the 70s and 80s and told from an almost godlike narrator that seems to know everything and everyone, and also has insight into everyone's future. If you're a beginning writer stick with third person until you feel more comfortable with point of view.

What POV to Use?

So how do you decide whose POV your story should be written in? For the beginning writer I'd say stick with just one and let all the action take place through their head and eyes. However, sometimes a story needs another voice. It might be to add a sub plot, or it could be to shed some light on one of your main characters.

The example here is from my upcoming story **Money Can't Buy You Love**. It's one of the early scenes and I wanted to show the reader that although Brock is somewhat of a playboy, he's all heart and I wanted to show that through his POV-

Brock checked the ad one more time. Yep, right place and if he wasn't mistaken the boat in question was the blue one that looked like… like it needed some work. However, that wasn't such a bad thing because it meant he'd have more wriggle room to negotiate a lower price. He walked along the dock until he reached the boat.

"Hello. Anyone on board?" he shouted.

A few minutes later a man in his seventies with grey hair and a beard appeared on deck.

"Can I help you?" he asked.

"Yes, I'm Brock. I phoned you about an hour ago about your boat for sale."

"Yes, that's right."

"I take it this is it?

"The one and only. You want to come on board and take a look around?"

"Sure, that would be great."

Brock jumped up on deck and shook his hand.

"My first question is why are you selling it?"

Brock took a quick look around. Yes, definitely needed some TLC which meant he could really offer much lower than the asking price.

"I don't want to. I love this old boat but it's my sister. She had a stroke last week. Doctors said she'll need to go into an assisted living home. Well, I can't have that. So I said I'd sell up and move in with her."

Brock suddenly felt a lump in his throat. Geez, what a nice guy to do something like that for his sibling.

"About the price?" began Brock.

"I know it's on the high side for what she is but I need all the money I can get to pay for my sister's hospital bill. She has Medicare but that doesn't pay for the half of it."

Brock swallowed the lump in his throat. Geez, if he was a hard nosed business guy like his dad, sob story or not, the guy would sell him this piece of junk for half the asking price and like it. However, Brock wasn't his father. He was a softy, a pushover and...

"No problem at all. I think she's worth every penny."

The old man held out his hand. "Do we have a done deal?"

"We sure do," said Brock shaking it.

When To Switch POV?

How do we know when it's time to switch POV in a story? Once again there are no rules but I think the more you know your characters before you sit down to write their story, the more you'll get a feel for whose head you want to be inside in any particular scene. (Remember the character sketch from the previous chapter?)

One question I ask myself when I'm thinking about switching POV is what should the reader know at this point of my story? For example, do they need to know that the hero in lying and keeping something major a secret from everyone...if that's the case that can only come from his POV?

The Dreaded Head Hopping Syndrome

One of the most common mistakes I see in many of my student's work is what's known as head-hopping. If you're not familiar with it, it's where a writer abruptly switches from one point of view to another in the space of a paragraph or even a few sentences. It's an especially big problem in a short story because of its length which makes head-hopping even more jarring for the reader. It's also a common reason for an editor to reject your work. However, the good news is it's one of the easiest mistakes to fix.

How Not to Be a Head-Hopper

The easiest way to avoid head-hopping is to tell the story from just one person's POV. However, that's not always possible because you need the story told through a second narrator to up the suspense or reveal something the main character couldn't possibly know themselves. My tip is to keep one POV per scene or if you can one POV per chapter.

One Tip Cures All

If you follow this rule you'll never make a head-hopping slip ever again. As you're writing your story think about our five senses. Remember that a character can physically *see* what another one's doing, *assume* what they're thinking, but they *can't* feel, taste, see, hear or think what another's feeling, tasting, seeing, hearing or thinking.

POV and Character

Remember about needing a great character to tell a story and having the reader relate to them? We do that through POV. In the chapter on characterization I told you that we all have similar fears, goals, things that makes us happy etc. For example, perhaps the character's wife has just walked out after twenty years of marriage or maybe her son is leaving for university and she's scared of being on her own for the first time. You want the reader to experience what's going through the heads of these two characters and not the wife or the son. Make the reader connect with the character and you've not only hooked an editor but won over lots of readers who think *I've felt that way too or I've thought that and I want to read on.*

POV and Emotion.

And yes, POV and emotion are connected. In fact, in a romance emotion is king. Through using their POV it's one of the easiest ways you can get your readers to both empathize and sympathize with your character. Once this relationship has been established and cemented it's easy to hook them so they turn the pages. Yes, even if the plot has been done a million times already.

Here's another example from **Money Can't Buy You Love**. Brock and Kate haven't known one another long and here through Brock's POV we learn more about Kate and gain sympathy for her, not through her own eyes but through someone else's-

Brock checked out the photos by the stairs. Looked like the

restaurant or at least the building in which it was housed had been around since the late eighteen hundreds. Even a few black and white shots hung on the wall. A branch tapping the window caught his attention and he glanced outside. It was getting darker by the minute, and by the look of the restaurant's sign, which was flapping back and forth, the wind had picked up too.

Kate had been upstairs for the last fifteen minutes. Maybe she couldn't find any spare sheets. He wanted to get back to the boat to make sure it was securely moored. He hoped she wouldn't mind him going up the stairs to find her.

By the time he got to the top, he heard her crying. He followed the sobs. Sounded like her heart was breaking. Maybe she'd gotten a phone call with bad news or something. He didn't want to impose, so he crept along the hallway. The door, to what he assumed was her bedroom, was half open and there she sat on the bed, holding what looked like a tablecloth on her lap.

He'd never known anyone get that emotional over one before, but maybe something else had set her off. She had her head down in her hands and even from the hallway he could see her shoulders bobbing up and down with each sob.

Brock wasn't sure what to do. His instinct told him to go comfort her, see what her tears were about, but he hardly knew her. And on top of that, she hadn't invited him up to her living area. This was private. He was intruding in her space and in her inner sanctum where she found it obviously safe and necessary to sit on her bed and have a good cry.

He'd forget about the sheets and get them some other time. He'd sleep on the mattress tonight and throw his jacket over him, no big deal. As he turned to go back downstairs a floorboard squeaked under his left foot. Damn, he didn't want to seem like a nosy neighbor so he hurried along the hallway and took the stairs down two at a time.

"Brock."

Obviously not quick enough…

POV and Plot

There will be certain things you'll want the reader to know and sometimes you have to decide how you're going to tell them. Whose POV would best convey that?

What POV Should I Use?

Most romances are written in third person past tense. If you're thinking about writing for any of the category romances published by Harlequin and Mills and Boon, that's the standard. However, once you get into more mainstream romances the choice is yours. Some people like first person while others hate it. I say give everything a try and see what you're more comfortable with.

Deep POV

And then there's something called Deep POV which really kicks a story into top gear. One definition has said that when the writer uses it, it's the equivalent of being a method actor. You emerge yourself totally in that character, inside both the head and heart. It's one hundred percent character. It took me some books to get into the habit of using deep POV for even just a few scenes, and now I wouldn't be without it. It's the element that can give your story that emotional punch and set it apart from other writer's work.

I know lots of people don't like to overdo it but I say go for it as much as you can. One common reason for a manuscript being rejected is the editor thinks you're guilty of author intrusion which means you the writer got in the way of the reader and the character. It's the *then he thought he heard sentences*. With Deep POV, the writer leaves the scene and the reader sees, hears, smells, feels everything that characters is seeing, hearing, feeling. I can't think of a better way to experience a story. No tags are present and the reader doesn't even notice you're telling them a story.

It will take some time to get used to going into deep POV and sometimes you're doing it without realizing it. Imagine if you will you are the character and you're telling your story, sharing with the reader everything that's going on in your life, your head and at the moment of the scene.

Scenes That Don't Work

I have lots of my students ask me what they can do about scenes that don't seem to be working no matter how many times they rewrite it. One tip I give is to switch POV to another one of your characters. Sometimes that's all it needs.

Key Points

POV in interconnected with all elements of the storytelling process.

POV can affect the reader's experience both good and bad.

POV can make a story more emotional.

POV can lessen or eliminate the distance between your character and reader.

POV is the person whose emotions, eyes, head, heart we experience the story through.

Something for you to try

Look at the book you're currently reading and read one chapter. Whose POV are you in and how can you tell?

Now try writing that chapter again but this time from another character's POV and see how things are change.

Chapter Five

Emotion

Emotion is a key element to all good stories. By evoking an emotion in your reader you can help them connect with your characters.

You probably won't find a whole chapter devoted to emotion in most writing books. Maybe not even other books about romance writing but I think it's vital to any story, whether it be a short story or four hundred page romantic family saga. Most of us want to feel something when we read a story, whether it be fear, laughter, or happiness. However, ask a romance reader the number one reason they love the genre so much and they'll tell you it's because they're packed with emotion.

Reason Romance Manuscripts Get Rejected

When I decided to switch from writing mysteries to romances the majority of my early rejections were due to one thing. I'd failed to put enough emotion into the story. At first I couldn't figure out what they meant. Did they want crying and sobbing or what? Then one day I sat down to write and suddenly figured out what the editors were getting at.

In a romance the reader wants to live vicariously through the heroine. Along with the heroine, she wants fall in love with the hero. And to do that you have to make her feel all the emotions that a real person feels when they meet the person of their dreams and fall in love.

So how do you do that?

Characterization

Yes, we're back to character again. The more life like you can make all the characters, but especially the heroine, the more chance you have of the reader stepping into her shoes to enjoy the story. She has to be likable and a good person but don't make her too perfect because no one in real life is. But she has to be someone that the reader considers worthy of the hero's love.

And speaking of the hero, he has to be likable too because this wonderful heroine who we now identify with, has fallen in love with him. He too can have his faults but the reader wants to know that he's going to make the heroine happy for the rest of her life.

Plot

I say never overdo the melodrama but some stories are better at packing an emotional punch than others. And once again the more true to life the story is the better the reader identifies with it and becomes emotionally engaged. We've all had our hearts broken at some point, maybe lost a job, or maybe lost a spouse. Maybe been in love with someone and it's not worked out but then they walk back into our lives and the whole emotional rollercoaster thing starts up again. Think back to those times in your life and how you felt. Inject that into both your story and the characters.

Here's an example of how I put lots of emotion into my story **One Night With You**. I've used it as an example of how you can play up emotion for not one but both main characters. This is from the hero's POV. We're experiencing his pain when he explains to the heroine why they've not been able to conceive, and also the fact that he's got to say goodbye to her so she can find another way to have a child. We feel and experience his pain and through his POV and also some of hers too-

"So maybe it's temporary. We could keep trying, right?"

He loved the hope and determination he heard in her voice,

but they had to be realistic. Or at least he had to be. Mike took Dana in his arms.

"Yeah, it's possible you could get pregnant at some point, but it could take a long time. I've come here to assure you that your not getting pregnant hasn't been your fault. And my second reason is to now give you a chance to find another man to father your baby."

She was crying now, almost breaking her heart by the sound of things. She was sobbing, her shoulders going up and down harder with each one. He wanted to soothe her pain, hold her, but right now he didn't think that was a smart idea because pretty soon he would be getting up and leaving her.

"I've set my heart on it being you. You'll make a great father," she managed to say through her tears and sobs, and it was tearing him apart.

He wasn't sure who this was harder on, him or her. He wanted to father her child more than anything, but by some awful twist of fate his body didn't want to cooperate.

"Dana, you made a wish. If you stick with me it's not going to come true."

"I know it will. We just have to give it more time. Please, let's try again and see what happens."

He shook his head. "I won't do this to you. I won't try and have a baby with you ever again."

She closed her eyes and sobbed some more. "That leaves me with the sperm bank and artificial insemination. You're the one who convinced me that's not the way I wanted to do this whole motherhood thing."

"I know it's cold and clinical, but at least you'll have your baby."

"I won't do it. It's either with you or nothing."

He couldn't let her do this. Ruin her dream. He grabbed both her arms and gave her a slight shake. He didn't want to hurt her, he never wanted to do that, but he'd have to talk some sense into her. She was going to make a great mother.

"Will you listen to me? You want a baby and you'll go to the sperm bank and pick out the best candidate for your child."

"You can't make me do it." She tried to wriggle out of his hands, but he held her still.

"Oh yeah, you want to bet? I told you what I hoped Todd was doing to your ex, having him pulled over, parking tickets, speeding tickets, you name it. You want me to arrange the appointment for you?"

He'd never spoken to anyone like this before and the last person he wanted to threaten in such a mean way was this beautiful woman he loved so much, but he had to do it for her own good. She'd see that eventually. When she held her baby for the first time.

"You couldn't do that to me." Her tear-soaked face was breaking his heart. He had to get out of here soon. He knew when he did that would have to be the last time he'd see her, be this close to her, touch her.

"Just try me. I want to hear you've made the appointment, picked out your sperm donor, and had the procedure done. Don't let us meet up at another New Year's Eve party and have me not see you with a baby bump."

He grabbed his jacket and headed for the door. He could hear her sobbing even after he'd shut her front door and stood on the doorstep for a few minutes trying to get his composure under control before he drove home. Mike knew he shouldn't have, but something deep inside him made him turn one last time to look at her townhouse as he got into his car. She was standing at the living room window watching him leave. She was sobbing, almost fighting for her breath, shoulders heaving. She put her hand on the glass. She mouthed his name, and before he turned away for the very last time he was sure she'd shouted she loved him.

Up the Stakes

As I mentioned before they aren't many rules when it comes to writing fiction but one is a must for all stories and that's conflict. Not people fighting and arguing non-stop but something that makes the reader uneasy and eager to turn the pages to see what happens the next. And in the case of romance the reason that the hero and heroine can't be together straight away.

There are two types of conflict, internal and external. Internal, stemming from the actual character is the way to go in a romance. I know it's not always easy to achieve internal conflict with every story, but when you do it packs more of an emotional punch.

The Dark Moment

If you're a romance reader you know there's a point in every story where things look hopeless and there's a good chance that these two people might not live happily ever after. This is the time to really up the emotional quota. This is the most likely spot in the story where the reader won't want to put the book down but need to continue reading to see what happens to the couple.

The Happy Ending

And on the other end of the emotional scale, there's joy and happiness that the reader will experience along with the characters as they put their differences aside. Conflicts are resolved and there's a satisfying ending and enjoyment that the reader takes away with them.

Key Points

Emotion is great in all stories but an essential element in romance stories.

One of the main reasons a romance story gets rejected is lack of emotion.

Remember back to times in your life when you broke up with

a boyfriend or someone you'd once loved waltzes back into your life and inject your feelings into those of your characters.

Emotions aren't all about loss and sadness, balance your stories with some joy and humor and remember the essential happy ending of the romance genre.

Something To Try

Look at the books you've read in the last couple of months, how was emotion handled in them. What made you sad, angry, happy while you read them?

Try writing your own emotional scene.

Chapter Six

Sexual Tension and Sexuality

You may or may not find sexual tension in genre likes sci-fi or mystery but in romances it's another must. In this chapter I'll show you ease ways to turn up the tension.

Depending on whether you're writing a romance where a kiss is as far as the couple goes or a more explicit one where anything goes and the language is more frank, there's one thing all romance novels have in common. In fact, it's their common denominator, and that's sexual tension. Without it, your manuscript is going to be rejected. So what is it and how do you incorporate it into your story?

Sexual tension doesn't have anything to do with the actual act of sex but it is everything that leads up to it. It's the first glimpse that the hero and heroine have of one another. He thinks, wow, she's gorgeous. She thinks, look at those baby blue eyes. There's an obvious attraction to one another but at the same time, something is keeping them from acting upon it.

That's the conflict.

It could be she thinks he's drop dead gorgeous but she's heard he's a lady's man and has had her heart broken one too many times by one of those types of guys so she stays clear of them.

But we writers like to complicate things so we keep bringing them into contact, and we continue to make them attracted just a little bit more each time they see one another. And then we push them in deeper. There's a kiss that looks like it's going to lead to more, but then both of them remember they don't want to get involved and they pull away leaving the reader feeling very uneasy.

And yes, we punish the couple more. We make the reader even more tense. We turn up the heat just a tad. The couple both think they're falling in love, but doubt still rattles around in their heads.

You get the picture. One of my writer friends likes to call this the *push and pull factor*. I couldn't describe it better. You push them together and then you pull them apart all the time while the reader is on the edge wondering how these two will get over their differences and admit they love one another. And depending on the type of book or line you're writing for; if they'll finally make love.

Here's an example of the push pull thing from my book **Last First Kiss** published by Evernight Publishing. The hero and heroine have a past history. She broke his heart and now she's been forced to come home to sort out a problem with her grandmother and realizes she never fell out of love with him but things can't be the way they were when she left-

She attempted to change stations again but Wade put his hand on top of hers. He obviously didn't do it to stop her because he just let his fingers rest on top of hers before running one of them over her knuckles. It tickled and felt good.

Sophie closed her eyes wanting to turn her hand over and hold onto his. He didn't move his hand when he said.

"Are you seeing anyone?"

She looked at him.

Why is he asking me that? Does he think there's still a chance for us?

"I've been seeing someone off and on for a couple of months but it's nothing serious, more friends than anything else."

It was true, she and David went out at least once a week but she never thought of him as serious boyfriend material and she guessed he felt the same way about her too. They were just two people who enjoyed one another's company every so often.

"How about you?" asked Sophie, not sure why she'd asked.

"I'm..."

Sophie looked at him, her heart slowly sinking because she knew what was coming next.

"I'm dating a woman who's not from Greenville. She just bought the beauty salon."

Sophie nodded and then looked out of the window. So he hadn't asked because he thought they'd get back together. He was just making polite conversation. And why would he want to renew a relationship with someone who'd committed the ultimate hurt.

"That's nice for you," she simply said, now unable to look at him.

"Her name's Cathy Moran. She's older than me, divorced and has a four year old boy."

She didn't answer, couldn't answer because she didn't want to hear about the woman who obviously had his heart. Sophie leaned her head against the pane of glass in the SUV and closed her eyes, almost on the brink of tears. Yeah, it was silly, but when it came to Wade...

"You okay, Sophie"

"Just tired."

"Why don't you take a nap? No snoring though."

She almost laughed, *almost*.

Sexuality Levels

Some romances don't even have one kiss, some stop at the bedroom door, while others are a continual romp between the sheets.

If writing about couples making love in explicit terms isn't your thing, I'd say stick with the sweeter romances. And if you're not comfortable writing slang terms and four letter words, I'd say erotic romances are definitely not for you.

My advice is to write what you're comfortable with because if you don't it's going to come across as awkward and that's the last thing you want an editor or reader to think about your writing style and story.

I've always written romances that are on the more spicy side so when erotic romances became popular I was in my element and had finally had the free reign to do more with the characters and to describe what really goes on between couples.

However, just because a sub genre is hot, don't jump in there just to try and make a sale. You won't write a good story because you'll be biting your nails worrying about how you're going to handle the up coming sex scene and your writing will suffer.

Write within your own comfort zone and you'll never go wrong and I'm betting your favorite type of story will be in fashion again one day soon.

Sexy Doesn't Have to Be About Sex

And if you think the not so spicy romances still can't be sexy, you'd be wrong. I've seen writers make characters and scenes come across the page as downright smoldering. Maybe it's the way the heroine tosses her hair back or the way the hero touches the side of her face and there's not one sex scene to be found in the entire book but you're still hot under the collar.

Writing With All the Senses

One thing all writers want to achieve is getting their readers to see, taste, hear, smell, and feel and experience everything the characters do during a story, and to do that you have to engage all the five senses.

What does the hero think of when he smells the heroine's hair? Is it flowers, something spicy...and how does it make him feel? Does it remind him of something else? Will he always think of the heroine when he smells something similar now?

And what about the hero's hands? How do they feel to the heroine the first time he slips his hand into hers and their palms touch?

Engage all the senses, do it in a sexy way and you've got sexual tension. You've upped the emotion and the reader can experience your story on a whole new level.

Key Points

Sexual tension is another must in a romance story.

Sexual tension doesn't have anything to do with the act of sex.

Some stories are full of sexual tension without having one sex scene.

Sexual tension relies on the push pull factor. They want to be with this person, they want to kiss them, but something is holding them back.

One way to create sexual tension is to write using all five senses.

Something for You to Try

Look through a romance novel and try to pick out a scene with lots of sexual tension. How did the writer handle it? Were any of the senses involved?

Try writing your own scene with as much sexual tension as you can pack into it.

Chapter Seven

Plot, Narration, Internal Thoughts and Pacing, Setting and Time

Stories aren't just about people and how they speak, scenes have to be connected and that's where narration factors in. And how you put together everything is like piecing together a jigsaw puzzle. How you tell it also effects the pacing of that story. In this chapter I'll also cover where your story is going to be set and when.

When you see the page of a book without much white space on it, there's a good chance you've stumbled upon a chunk of narration in the story. It's the places where the characters aren't speaking but they could be thinking about something that has happened or is about to happen. You could be in the character's head, it could be description about a place, or another character, but it helps link the story together.

Pacing

Pacing is the way the story reads. Have you ever heard someone say, I liked the book but I gave up on it because the pacing was too slow? (Very seldom do you hear the opposite but it can happen).

In fact, slow pacing can earn you rejection for an otherwise good story with interesting characters. So how can you make sure you're not guilty of painfully slow pacing?

I like to think of stories as recipes. If you had just one or two ingredients in a dish, it wouldn't be very appetizing. The same goes for a story. If you have all narration, all description and little dialogue, the reader's going to get bored quickly and stop reading.

Composing any story is like being a master chef and adding a little of this and a little of that, and knowing when to blend things together for the perfect creation.

Here's a tip I always share with my workshop participants and I've found it works for me so I hope you'll give it a try too.

On the first draft I like to think if the story was a human being I was putting together...a little like Dr. Frankenstein... on my first attempt I create the skeleton. On the second draft I add the skin and the muscles. On my final draft I add the blood and heart that makes the person, or in this case, the story, come to life.

It's like layering elements and I've found when you do that you're most likely to get the right mix of all the elements that makes a story good and the pacing right.

Here's an example of narration from **One Night With You** to show character and a little back story-

Mike dropped the razor into the sink, watching the blood from the nick on his face splash onto the white porcelain sink.

Second time he'd cut himself this evening.

He examined the damage. Just a year ago this would have been a piece of cake but these days he couldn't shave without getting at least one nasty nick. Maybe his hand needed more therapy. In the rehabilitation center they'd made him use an electric razor but he hated those damn things. Never could get the close shave he liked. Another drop of blood appeared on his face. Mike dabbed it with a tissue.

Maybe he should just forget about shaving tonight or his face would be covered in cuts by the time he was done. Probably a sign he shouldn't go to the party. He hated them anyway. Small talk, a few drunks, always the odd obnoxious person or two and the ones who couldn't mind their own business. He disliked those types the most.

However, Todd would probably keep phoning if he didn't

show up there. He knew his work buddy was making sure he wasn't spending his first New Year's Eve since the divorce all by his lonesome. Yeah, he couldn't fault the guy for thinking about him.

He splashed his face with some aftershave, grimacing when it found both cuts. Shit, that burned like hell but nothing as bad as being shot. Still he'd had enough pain this year to last him a lifetime. If he could get by without so much as a paper cut for the rest of his days he'd be a happy man.

Mike walked into his bedroom and opened the closet door. He'd forgotten to ask Todd if jeans and a sweater would be okay attire or if they were going the dressy route tonight. Mike picked up his cell phone to call him but instead threw it down on the bed. He wasn't in a dressing up type of mood so jeans it would be and they'd have to like it.

He combed his hair, slipped on his overcoat and turned off the lights. He'd stay for a few hours so it didn't seem rude him not showing up but after that he'd head home and see the clock turn time into a another year all by his lonesome.

And an example of narration to introduce a character from my work in progress **Amortal-**

Shit, what a crappy day it had been. The fog had cleared but now it sounded like a storm was moving in because Charlotte could hear rain or possibly sleet hitting the metal drainpipe outside the window. She'd moved to the Pacific Northwest just over six months ago to escape the East Coast's nasty winters but now Seattle was experiencing a wetter and colder one than normal. She noticed some of the rain bouncing off the window and hitting a pile of paper towels inside the room.

She rushed over to close it just as a plane heading for Sea Tac loomed overhead. It shook several boxes of Band Aids off the shelf and onto the floor. She bent over to pick them up and as she stood and piled them back into the cupboard, Charlotte got a whiff of the vomit that had now dried to a heavy crust on her lab coat. The first patient of the afternoon session had been a three year old boy who'd thrown up while she'd been examining him. She thought she'd managed to clean it all up but now realized some still remained and it had set like cement on the coat. She took it off, threw into the laundry bin, wondering why she'd taken this job. She'd given up her job and apartment in Boston and headed out to work at a Seattle area hospital only to find they'd given her position to someone else.

Charlotte had hated the thought of going back East, trying to find some place to live, to work, the endless snow laden winters, so as a last resort she'd accepted the position at the free clinic. The previous doctor had quit all of a sudden citing medical reasons for his abrupt departure. The position had opened up at the right time because she'd been just hours away from picking up the phone and booking her flight home.

Checking herself in the mirror by the door, Charlotte noticed there was some vomit on her skirt too. She needed to buy groceries on the way home and doubted other shoppers at the supermarket would appreciate the odor when she passed by. It was close to the end of clinic hours. There'd been no more patients in the waiting area when she'd headed back to the supply room, so she'd spend the last few minutes of her work day cleaning, or at least attempting to clean up her skirt.

She unzipped it, lowered it over her hips and placed the skirt over the sink and then dabbed at the vomit with a damp wash cloth. Just what had that little guy been eating? The vomit was bright green and almost impossible to remove from the ridges of the skirt's material. No wonder his mom had rushed him in here so quickly.

Charlotte sensed she was no longer alone. Someone was standing behind her watching her. Damn it, she hoped it wasn't a patient because she was only wearing her blouse and panties right now.

Someone coughed, no correct that, a man cleared his throat behind her.

Where to Set Your Romance Story

You might already have an idea where your story will take place. Some people choose their own country, state/county, or city but don't ever let that limit you. I've often written about places I've never been. However, a word of caution. Do research about it first because readers can be picky about any blaring mistakes you make about their hometown, or even what the weather's like in a certain month. When I started writing I'd get books from the library but now you can use the Internet and gain even more first-hand knowledge. Most towns have with own Web sites, and tourist offices will send you out books and brochures so there's no excuse about not getting something right. And check out the Weather Channel site and type in the name of the city or place you're writing about to get the weather forecast. One other resource is to ask your fellow writers if any of them reside in the area where your story is set. What better insider information than a local resident?

How to Choose the Setting

So where should your romance be set? I think anywhere you're comfortable writing about. It could be a big city like New York or the English countryside. And it doesn't necessarily have to be somewhere romantic like Paris or Venice.

And What About Time?

Are you only interested in writing romances set in modern day or would you like to travel back to the days of Vikings, Tudors or during the Regency? If you're a history buff as well as a writer, what better way to combine the two hobbies than writing an historical romance? Once again, the Internet has some great sites you can check out. You can even find historical societies and groups that have members that are more then willing to help you out with questions you might have.

Accuracy in Time and Setting

As I mentioned before some readers and yes, editors too, can spot blaring mistakes in stories with inaccurate historical detail so it not only pays to do research before you write, but after you've finished the book too. It's all too easy to get events out of sequence. And nothing loses credibility more than having your character switching on a light before electricity came to be.

Key Points

Check for accuracy for things like weather and historical detail.

The Internet is a great resource for beginning research before and during the writing process.

The perfect story has the ideal mix of dialogue and narration.

Slow pacing can put a reader off finishing an otherwise good story.

Think like a chef and add the right mix of ingredients for the perfect dish, your story.

Layer your story on each draft.

Something for You to Try

Take a section of a book with lots of dialogue and change it to narration. Then take a section with narration and turn it into dialogue between the characters in that scene.

Compare how the two sounded. Did it change the pacing?

Chapter Eight

Writing The Cover Letter and Synopsis

One thing lots of writers hate doing is writing a synopsis. It's something you have to get used to and they really can be fun. I teach a class on the topic and by the end of it most of my students say they no longer hate the task, so I hope you'll think the same way after reading this chapter.

The Cover Letter

Depending on the publisher's requirements sometimes a cover letter might be all you can send to get them interested in looking at your story. Just like going on an interview, you get one shot at creating a good first impression, so make sure your cover letter is word perfect.

Tell them briefly about your story and why you think it's a good fit for their publishing company. Keep it professional and don't, like some writers, go off on tangents saying your aunt loved it, or that your friends at work read it twice and think you're the next JK Rowling. You'll have a page or two at the most to sell your story, so stay focused. Tell the editor what makes it unique and why should the editor spend time reading it? Also, include any writing experience you have. And don't worry if you don't, just downplay it and keep all the focus on the story itself.

I always end my cover letters with a thank you for reading it and hope to hear from your soon notation. And leave it alone a few days before you send it out or hit the send button. You'll be surprised how many typos you can find or something that doesn't read quite right when you let it sit for awhile. Better yet have someone else read it for you.

Cover Letter With Synopsis

If you're sending a cover letter along with a synopsis, cut down on the amount of story you share with the editor. Just round it up and focus on the key points. Who and what is it about? You want to answer the editor's main concern when she opens it. Why should I be bothered to read this synopsis when I have one hundred others waiting for my attention?

The Importance of a Synopsis

I like to think of the synopsis as the writer's sales letter. Learning to write a great synopsis isn't just about catching an editor's eye. In fact, there are a couple more reasons to invest in honing this skill.

It's a New Publishing World

These days it's more important than ever to know how to write not just a so-so synopsis but a great one. While many publishers have closed their doors to unsolicited manuscripts, they still accept a query letter and synopsis. Submit a dazzling one and you can entice the editor into wanting to see sample chapters or even your complete manuscript. With just a few pages of work you've opened doors still closed to other writers.

And there are two more reasons that writing a great synopsis is an added plus for even published writers-

Number One

Once you've got a couple of books under your belt some publishers will invite you to submit a proposal for your next one. This might be a synopsis or it could be the synopsis and three chapters. Many will offer you a contract based on just this sample package. Yes, that's right; you don't have to write the whole manuscript and waste time putting together a story that may never sell. One of my publishers lets 'in house authors' send two such proposals to them at a time. We have to submit a synopsis and the first 2500 words. Many of my now published stories got their start this way.

Number Two

This one depends on whether or not you're a writer who likes to pen the synopsis first or after you've finished the manuscript. For some writers who always face the sagging middle or the plot that suddenly goes nowhere, a synopsis can keep or get you back on track.

The Perfect Synopsis

The perfect synopsis always makes the reader want to see the actual story. It convinces them they want to get to know the characters you've described, and to see how the plot you've told them about plays out.

Get To The Nitty-Gritty

Many writers get anxious about their synopsis because they feel they sound boring and read like a book report. Well, in a way, they should. There's a fine balance you have to strike between just stating the facts of the story, but doing it in a way that will make the reader sit up and take notice. What I'm about to tell you goes against the number one rule you've been told when it comes to penning a story...show don't tell. I've found the secret to writing the synopsis is the reverse, tell don't show.

And why? Most agents and editors request either a 1-2 page or 3-5 page synopsis, you've got to condense sometimes a 50-70,000 word story into that small space. There's no room for anything other than the facts of the story.

Editors don't have a lot of time because they have deadlines to meet and meetings to attend, so the quicker you can show them that this is the story they want to see the better it is for you.

Focus On The Key Players

The good synopsis keys in on the major players. The first focus should always be your main character or characters. In a genre like romance, the editor will be most concerned about your hero and heroine, so don't waste time or precious page space on characters that aren't major players or have no bearing on your story or the hero and heroine. For example, the girl that works with heroine unless she's going to introduce her to Mr. Right or steal Mr. Right doesn't need to be included.

Key In On The Conflict

A good synopsis tells the reader all about the conflict. Remember the number one rule of writing captivating fiction, if there's no conflict, there's no story. Same goes for the synopsis, show the reader what the problem is and what these characters face during the story.

Give Away The Plot

A good synopsis explains to the reader the major plot twists, the unexpected turn of events, such as the hero is really on the run from the law, the heroine was married before…you get the picture.

Tell Them the Bad Stuff

The perfect synopsis tells the reader about the black moment. That section in the story where things look bleak and you feel there's no way these two people can ever be together or the main character is going to die.

Never Be a Tease

A good synopsis never teases the reader. I've heard so many editors complain about writers who leave an open ending and write *I bet you want to know how this one ends, if so I'll send you my manuscript.* Don't be amateur. Always show them how you as a skilled writer will tie up all lose ends and resolve everything so these people can have their happily ever after.

Remember Your Sub Genre

A great synopsis is story specific. Paranormal needs more background to convey the world and people you've created because it doesn't exist in the real world. Romantic suspense needs more attention to timeline and sequence of events.

What Tense Should I Use?

The most common question I get asked during a workshop is what tense should the synopsis be written in? I don't think there are any written rules but the most common is present tense. It's the easiest and I think gets the job done effectively.

What About Stories Told in First Person?

Some of you might be writing a story that's told in the first person and wonder if you should use it in the synopsis. The answer is no, third person is the way to go.

Should I Include Dialogue?

My answer would be no but there is one exception and I used it in my synopsis for my mystery **Death Likes Me**. I didn't include it in the body of synopsis but quoted the first sentence of the story to lead into it. Why did I choose to do it? The story is told in the first person and I thought this one piece of dialogue...well, it's actually an internal thought, would get their attention. So if the opportunity arises where you begin your story will something you think will help set the stage for your story, or even insight into your main character's motivation, I say go for it and use it.

How About Bold Print?

One thing I've been doing for the last few years is putting the key characters' names in bold print the first time I mention them. I think it makes them stand out to the reader.

When Should I Write Synopsis?

The answer is there is no set rule. Sometimes I won't write one until after I've typed the period at the end of my story. Other times I'll have a very detailed one written before I sit down to compose. The deciding factor for me is how long the story's been in my head. Sometimes I'll go for months thinking about a plot or certain characters and start making notes which become my synopsis. Other times I'll just sit and start writing and have no idea where a story's going until the characters take me there.

I don't think it's any easier to write it before or after and it's a very individual thing. My advice would be to try both ways and see what's easier for you.

The Exceptions

Having said that I think there are some situations where you will need to write the synopsis before you start the story-

Submitting to a Publisher or Agent

I mentioned that some publishers will only allow you to send in a synopsis if you don't have an agent. Don't let this opportunity pass you by. This is your chance to put the wheels in motion on your path to getting the story in print. It also allows you to see if the story will grab an editor's attention. Remember they're just 'hearing' about the story, not how you write. If they reject it at this point it could be either you've not done a good job with the synopsis, or it could be that the story isn't feasible because it's been done a million times etc.

The Story is Long or Has Suspense or Mystery Elements

Writing the synopsis before you begin the manuscript is essential if you write intricate plots, stories in the 70,000 word range, romantic suspense, lots of characters etc. It allows you to keep track of plot lines and who's where, who's been killed, set out clues etc. It makes the whole experience that much easier.

You Get Lost Easily

Some writers and this happens not only to beginning writers but established ones too, you don't know where the story is going next and things come to a screaming halt. Some manuscripts even fall by the wayside never to be worked on again. If that describes you then I recommend writing a synopsis before you start the story.

Synopsis Template

For me anything that makes writing easier is a plus. For the last year or so I've worked with a synopsis template that I hope will help you too. I have this stored on my computer and when it's time to write I just fill in the blanks and add a synopsis.

Synopsis for (title of manuscript)
Author name
Pen name (if any)
Contact information (always include this here as well as your cover letter...you'd be surprised how often things get lost)
Genre and sub genre
Setting
Time Period
Sensuality Level (optional)
Word Count
Synopsis- Here I lead into the actual synopsis

Okay, let's go through some elements of the template. I think setting the information out like this helps the reader see at a glance what you're offering. Remember I said editors are busy. This is a way to make their jobs easier, gets you remembered and in their good books.

Genre

I include genre and sub-genre (if any), be as specific as you can...the reason is to your advantage. An editor or agent might be looking for something very specific the day they open your mail or e-mail. Maybe an editor realizes time travel novels are selling well again and it just so happens your synopsis falls on the agent's desk or even this editor's desk that very day. They didn't need to read through all the manuscripts hoping to find a time travel story, yours was clearly displayed.

Setting and Time

Always put where the book is set and also the time period, is it contemporary? If it's historical get specific, New England, 1775 etc.

Word Count

Word Count is very important, never leave this out...I sometimes mention it in my cover letter too but just in case the two get separated, include it in your synopsis.

Formatting your Synopsis

One last tip I have is to make sure that you have a space between each paragraph in your synopsis. As these are single spaced, the short breaks make it easier on the reader's eye. It also helps you proofread. Font size- I stick with 12 point and as there is no fast and hard rule on font type I go with the most generic which seems to be Times Roman.

Key Points

The cover letter is sometimes you only chance to make a good first impression.

The synopsis is one of the basic and must have skills for the writer.

The synopsis can open doors to publishers and agents who won't look at sample chapters or complete manuscripts.

Present tense and telling and not showing is often the best way to write one.

Something for You To Try

Here's something that I hope will help you figure out what's important in a synopsis and what's not. For this one I don't want you to focus on your own story... The reason behind this is when we create a story we think everything is important and lose sight of the most relevant things. We all do it but hopefully this exercise will have you thinking in a different way.

What are you reading right now? What have you read recently? Pick a book, think about the storyline and write a synopsis based on it. You can post it to the group for feedback or use it for your own reference. While you're writing it I want you to think about the following-

1　Why you chose to include certain things
2　Was there anything that happened in the story that while interesting you didn't think it should be included in the synopsis? Why?
3　In your synopsis what did you reveal about the characters?
4　How about plotlines and turns? What did you think was interesting enough for us to hear about?
5　Obviously this is a published book and piqued someone's interest but now play editor or agent. Read through the synopsis and ask yourself would I request the manuscript after reading this synopsis? If the answer is no, what do you think you can add or subtract to grab a reader's attention?

Chapter Nine

Romance Sub Genres

Remember in the first chapter I told you about all the various sub genres of romance? In this chapter I'll cover each one, what it is and some authors who have made their names in those areas.

Category Romances

I probably don't have to say much about category romance because the name of Mills and Boon and Harlequin jump at you immediately. Many big name authors who continually find themselves on the bestseller's list got their start in category romance. People like Janet Evanovich, Lisa Jackson, Debbie Macomber and Brenda Novak to name a few.

Many beginning romance writers target one of the category lines for their first attempt and with good reason. In each of the lines they publish four or six books per month which means they need lots of stories. Combine that with the fact that some of their authors move onto mainstream books and new openings emerge all the time. That isn't to say that it's any easier to get published. I tried these markets for years before realizing my writing wasn't suited to these types of books.

However, if you're an avid reader of any of their lines, I'd say give one a try because it could be a perfect fit. Here are some pros and cons of writing for category romance-

Pros

You're given specific guidelines and word count so you have a basic outline to work from.

They're an already established line with a built in readership and fan base. Some readers buy all the books in a line every month.

No agent is required. You have lots of different categories to choose from, everything from historical romance to medical ones so there's bound to be something that's a good match for you.

Cons

The writing is more rigid because you have to conform to the standards for that line which isn't always a good thing, if like me you like to try something a little different. And because they have so many other books to compare your story to sometimes you're rejected because you're not hitting all the right targets.

Romantic Suspense

If you like a little mystery and suspense with your romances, this might be a good fit for you. Some books are more suspense than romance and vice versa. Some are fondly known as a woman in jeopardy, where the heroine might have married a man who seems to be up to no good and her life's in danger. Or it could be the heroine who's stumbled upon something she shouldn't have and now the bad guys are chasing her. In this category you can also find gothic romances, although their popularity seems to have waned in recent years, a comeback might be on the horizon. Some bestselling authors to check out in this category are Brenda Novak, Lisa Gardner, Heather Graham, Lisa Jackson, Sandra Brown and Catherine Coulter.

Historical Romances

If you don't like setting your romances in modern times than penning an historical romance might be your cup of tea. If could the set in 14th century Scotland, France during the Revolution, England during the Second World War, or even ancient Rome. There's also another sub genre that falls in this category and that's Regency romances or historicals set during the Regency. Both remain firm favorites with readers.

Bestselling authors to check out in this category include, Lisa Kleypas, Patrica Gaffney, Mary Balogh, Jo Beverely, and Julia Quinn.

Time Travel Romance

Who doesn't remember the movie Somewhere in Time starring the late Christopher Reeves? Or even the more recent The Time Traveler's Wife? Either the hero or the heroine travel back or forward in time and most of the conflict stems from that very fact. Can they both live together in one another's time or will they suddenly be transported back never to see their true love again?

Bestselling authors to check out are Diana Gabaldon's Outlander books and Susanna Kearsley.

Paranormal Romances

Time travel does fall under this category too, and also the vampire romances, werewolves, shape shifters, ghosts, and witches, you name it. Although their popularity is leveling off, they do remain firm favorites with fans especially in the US market.

Bestselling authors to check out include- Laurell K Hamilton and Sherrilyn Kenyon.

Inspirational Romances

Harlequin has a couple of lines of inspirational romances like Love Inspired and also Bethany House specializes in them. Characters are Christian. Authors to check out include-Beverly Lewis and Karen Kingsbury.

Steampunk, Sci fi, and Fantasy

I've grouped these three categories together because there is some overlap to what's contained in these stories. Steampunk is sci-fi mixed with alternate history which takes place during the

Victorian age. It mixes historical elements with technology and if you can't quite understand what that is then if you remember the old TV show or the more recent movie The Wild Wild West, you know what steampunk is? Authors to check out include M.K Hobson and Gail Dayton.

Urban Fantasy

If you ever watched Buffy The Vampire Slayer, you know what an urban fantasy is. It's a kick ass heroine who is definitely a match for the hero. As she's falling in love she's tackling vampires, werewolves and other things that go bump in the night.

Authors to check out are Laurell K Hamilton.

Erotic romance

Excuse the pun. but since the emergence of the electronic book market, erotic romances have been the hot sub genre of the romance market. And print and big name publishers seem to be catching on to their popularity because many have recently added their own erotic romance lines. Authors to check out are Portia Da Costa.

Chick Lit

Bridget Jones' Diary. Those three words should tell you exactly what chick lit is. Although once a very, very hot sub genre, chick lit is waning. However, if it's something you enjoy writing, then it's worth trying but just put a new spin on it, and who's to say when it won't be the pick of the bunch again. Check out authors such as Sophie Kinsella.

Women's Fiction

I can't close out this chapter without some mention of women's fiction because many books do contain a romantic element and in some books you'll see the spine does read romance. It could be anything from a sweeping family saga that spans centuries, or a book with a romantic sub plot. Either way the books are aimed at the female reader. Authors to check out Barbara Taylor Bradford and Maeve Binchy.

Something for You To Try

Not sure which sub genre you'd like to write? Visit the library and check out a couple of books in each category. Then when you've narrowed it down, read as many books in that genre as you can to get a feel for the language and style.

Chapter Ten

Electronic Markets

These days no book about writing of any sort would be complete without a chapter on the electronic market. With the birth of both the Kindle and Nook, it's a market that will continue to grow. And once again, it's the romance genre that's seen the biggest market share. While other genres like mystery and non-fiction are catching up, romance and its many off shoots remain reader favorites. My own writing career had a second launch because of e-books and I can honestly say it's a fun, exciting, and ever expanding market to write for so I encourage you to check it out.

What's an electronic book?

An e-book, as they're known is just the same in content as its print cousin but it's both *printed* and read in an electronic format. It could be on your computer, on your Kindle, even on your phone. Some publishers offer both print and electronic books, while some are exclusively paperless. Some of the first e publishers include romance markets such as Ellora's Cave based in Ohio, USA.

Writing e-books and its Advantages

Writing an e-book is no different to penning one for the print market. You need all the same skills and qualities that publishers and editors expect in paper form. And should you sell a story to one, you'll be required to work on edits to improve and polish your story just as you would with a traditional publisher.

Why Work With an E-Book Publisher

There are many advantages to choosing to write for the electronic market. If you're a first time author you stand a better chance of being published in electronic format than paper. One because the market is in a growth pattern and more writers are needed. Two, very few if any, electronic publishers require you to have an agent in order to submit.

Everything is sent via e-mail so you can save money on postage and printing costs too. Responses (and yes, rejections) come your way quicker too.

Your book will get to the market much faster, and sometimes you'll be paid monthly instead of quarterly. Contracts are signed electronically and royalties can usually be paid into a PayPal account. And because publishers are saving on print costs it usually means higher royalties for the writer.

Disadvantages

If you're someone who once published would like to physically hold a book in your hand or sign it at your local book store, electronic books can't offer that.

Another drawback is books are more likely to be pirated. Although the industry is working on ways to stop people from buying and then downloading or selling your work.

Where to sell your work

The number of electronic publishers continues to grow daily but it pays to be cautious. Some have already closed their doors and many writers have found themselves owed money. Check out a publisher before you submit work to them, and definitely before signing a contract with them.

Electronic contracts range from anywhere from two to seven years and royalties ranging from anywhere from 35-60%. If you do a Google search you'll find a long list. Some of the bigger ones include Samhain, Carina Press (Harlequin's electronic format) and Loose ID in the US and Xcite Books in the UK.

What to Expect from Working with an E-Publisher

Working with an e-publisher is the same as working with print one. You need to be professional, handle and return edits to your editor's deadlines and work with your editor to produce a book both of you can be proud of. Edits are done electronically and sent through e-mail. Usually you'll get two or three edits. Sometimes they go to a line editor and then come back to you for your okay.

Most of them won't let you pick your book cover but you do have more of say in how it looks than with a print publisher. Many times they'll have you fill in form describing your hero and heroine and the setting of the story.

What To Avoid

Many e-publishers are springing up and sometimes they're a one person operation that opens its doors hoping to make it rich by taking advantage of the ever growing market only to go out of business when the million dollars doesn't come their way in the first year of business. The great thing is you can do a lot of checking online. First of all check out their Web site. How many books have they published? How about the authors? Some might not be familiar to you but it shouldn't just be books by the owner and a few of their friends. And books covers; do they look professional? Covers really do sell any book whether it's print or e-book so it pays to get with a publisher who hires professional designers. And how about editing? I have seen some books that have blaring mistakes and typos that should have been caught. My advice is to check out some of their titles and give them a read. Not only to see what they're publishing but how the book looks and is edited too.

Key Points

The electronic market is growing at incredible speed and can be the perfect market for the beginning writer.

Just because a book won't be published in print doesn't mean you don't have to be professional in your attitude toward edits and deadlines.

Be cautious about signing a contract. Check out the publisher thoroughly.

Something for You To Try

Visit a site like Amazon and click on Kindle store to see what books are being published.

Chapter Eleven

Time to Submit Your Romance Story

I know I might be jumping ahead here but some of you might already have a manuscript that's waiting to go out or close to being ready. And of course the rest of you who are reading the book are going to sit down at the computer and start writing, right? So this chapter is all about that first step to selling your manuscript and that's submitting it.

Places to Sell your Story

In the opening chapter you'll remember I told you that romance is the best selling genre and for that reasons you have more markets to submit work to. Depending on what type of story you want to write will determine what markets open to you.

After reading the previous chapter do you want to work in category romance? If so, the first thing to do is get the writer's guidelines, most of them are available online now. And see where your story will be a good fit, or maybe you've even written the story for a specific line in mind, like Harlequin Blaze.

If you're more of a mainstream romance writer you'll need to look at publishers who don't require an agent such as Avon, Kensington, etc.

One good resource is Writer's Market which updates its listing each year. Also do a search online and you'll find the publisher's Web site. Check on either *submissions, write for us,* or failing that, *about us or contact us*. If you don't see any send information about submissions send an e-mail to their general inquiry address.

Check Out The Publisher You're Targeting

So many publishers have different requirements about submissions that one thing you need to do is check before submitting. Most have separate pages for this and will tell you if you need an agent or if they just require a synopsis etc. Do your homework; don't skip over this part because it not only wastes their time but yours too. Some even have most of them have specific requirements about formatting, for example some want Times Roman, some what Bookman, etc. My advice is if they don't spell out anything in particular go with a Times Roman or Courier, 12 point which are the two most common ones.

Okay now down to the specifics-

Indent each paragraph

Put a new chapter on a separate page

Scene switch within a chapter ***** or whatever mark the publisher uses

Dialogue should be on a separate line, also indented

Some require headers and page numbers so once again check their requirements.

Final Editing

Give your manuscript time to sit before you give it a final read through and edit. You'll be surprised how many mistakes you'll find. Read it aloud. You'll get a sense of rhythm. Ask yourself if you've varied sentence length. There should also be a mix of long and short sentences.

Main Reasons for Rejection

There are lots of reasons for an editor rejecting your work and some of them are kind enough...yes, I say kind enough to tell you what you've done wrong so you can correct it on your next attempt. If you don't get that feedback here are the most common reasons I've found over my years writing-

Not the sort of story that the publisher wants right now.

Sloppy proofreading and grammar etc.

Lack of emotion

Flat and cardboard characters who the editor couldn't relate to
Over hackneyed plot
Blaring inconsistencies in the plot
Information dumping in the first chapter.

Critique Partners and Getting Feedback

One thing you might want to do is look for a fellow writer to pair with to give and get feedback on your story. Finding a good critique partner is almost as tough as getting published. At least it was for me. They really are worth their weight in gold and don't worry if it takes you awhile to find the right one. Sometimes you think someone's perfect and they're not, or you never hear back from them again. But just like getting published; don't give up if the first couple of attempts don't work out.

A critique partner can be your second pair of eyes for finding typos that you were convinced never existed. They can point out where things are consistent, for example your main character was Cade in the first three chapters and now he's suddenly Kade or Wade. Or the town was called Bellingham in chapter one and now in chapter five it's mysteriously turned into Billingham. They can put out when you use the same word too many times or if the plot doesn't sound realistic enough. They can also be a sounding board if you're having trouble working on a story and need a second head to figure out how to fix or change something.

There are lots of ways to find critique partners. Some of my students team up during workshops, and I've listed some sites to check in the resource section that I hope are helpful to you.

Do You Need an Agent?

I'll be honest up front. I'm not the biggest fan of agents because the experience I've had with them hasn't been that great. Many times selling to a publisher is a lot easier than getting an agent to represent you especially when you're new to publishing. However, some writers do find it's their ideal route to publication.

If you're looking for an agent, make sure they're a member of the Association of Authors' Representatives. They shouldn't charge you a fee for reading your work. If you are offered a contract make sure you understand the terms including the length of the contract and the percentage they'll take for representing you. Ask for monthly updates on the places they're sending your work and the feedback they're getting if your work isn't selling. Check out other writers they represent and ask for some honest feedback about the agent. Like every other profession there are some bad apples and having an awful agent can sometimes be worse than not having one, so do your homework.

Entering Contests

You see a writing contest advertised. You have the perfect entry, so should you go for it?

From a personal viewpoint, I'd have to say yes. Writing contests have been good to me. In fact, the first money I ever earned as a writer, all $250 of it, was from winning a contest. And here are some other reasons why I think they're worth your effort.

You Get a Deadline

You might just be toying with the idea of being a writer or have a story floating around in your head but never seem to get down to writing it. However, by entering a contest there's a deadline so that story get's written. It might be just the motivation that you need.

Free Critiques

Well, if the contest has an entry fee it's not really free but some contests will send you the judges' reports and you can get an honest appraisal, not only of the story, but your overall writing ability too. They might point out what you're doing wrong and hopefully what you can do to correct it.

Your Work Gets Read by People in the Business

Some contests are judged by real editors which means a professional reads it, and who knows might like it enough to see more.

You Earn Some Money

If like me you win, you get money for your time and effort and yes, even a publishing contract could be on the cards too.

Chapter Twelve

Finding Time to Write and Dealing With Rejections

In this final chapter I'll offer you ways to find time to write, even on your busiest days. And how to handle what will be an inevitable part of your writing life, the dreaded rejection.

Make Time to Write

With our automated, almost paperless world it would seem we have more time on our hands, but that's not always the case. Many students tell me the most difficult thing for them is not the actual writing but finding time to squeeze it in after a day's work and family commitments. While not all these tips work for everyone, I hope you'll find one or two that will come in handy.

Write Every Day

Writing it a lot like being an athlete in training. To get to a competing level you've got to train and practice every day. But don't panic if there are days that go by when you can't squeeze in a few hours or even one. On *one those days* and yes, we all have them, just aim for a few paragraphs. My advice is something is better than nothing. Don't get angry or frustrated if you miss a day but just promise yourself you'll get back on track.

Be a Time Keeper

Use your time wisely, even if you're not writing make notes about plots, characters, even if it's for a different story than the one you're currently working on.

Be Realistic

Sometimes you have to give up something else but if you've set your heart on writing a book so it shouldn't be much of a sacrifice. For me, that sometimes means less time gardening or reading.

Make A Date

Put it on your calendar as something you *have* to do.

Rejections...yes they can be good for you

If there's one downside to writing it's receiving a rejection and yes, even bestselling authors get them so never feel bad. Rejections are an inevitable part of being a writer. They never get easier but I have found some pluses that I'd like to share with you as a parting word to you and I hope you'll remember back to these on days you feel like quitting.

You're Actually a Writer

Lots of people talk about writing but never get down to actually doing any composing. Getting a rejection means you've written something and had the courage to send it out and show the world you mean business. You've taken that first step to being a published writer so you should be proud.

Rejections Can be a Gauge of Your Writing Skills

When I first started out my rejections were the standard kind... *dear writer, unfortunately this isn't right for us*...However, they eventually changed to the personal kind with the editor adding handwritten notes at the bottom telling me why it didn't work for them. And after that the rejections became even more detailed... this isn't for us but you're obviously a talented writer and we'd like to see your next story etc.

These might seem like just rejections but they show how you're growing as a writer and that you're heading in the right direction.

Rejections are a Free Critique

In the early days I used to think if only they'd tell me why they didn't like my story. Editors are busy and few will tell you, but yes, some will be kind enough to do it, so think of it as a plus and learn from what they say about your manuscript. Does it have flat characters or slow pacing? You'd pay a lot of money to get a critique from someone in the business so use the feedback to your advantage.

You can Get to Know an Editor

If you keep sending work to the same editor…yes, I've done it, many get to know you and some even offer encouragement because they realize that you're in this for the long haul and willing to work at your craft.

They Make You a More Determined and Better Writer

Maybe it's just me but every time I get a no, sorry, this isn't for us, I became that much more determined that the next one will be a yes; we'd love to offer you a contract.

I wish you the very best as you sit down to write your romance novel. I teach workshops throughout the year at various places on the Web and I'd love to 'see' you in one of them some day soon. You can check out at my schedule at www.thiswriterslife.com I also love to hear from fellow writers and I can be reached at suspalm2@gmail.com

Happy writing and thank you for buying this book.

Resources

Writing Dialogue

To Get a Feel For What Makes Great Dialogue, scripts are a wonderful resource.

To purchase a screenplay visit http://store.scriptbuddy.com/browse/screenplays/

Writer's Organizations

There are lots of writer's groups and organizations you can join. I've found some are more worthwhile than others and lot depends on where you're at in your career. Check out what you get for your membership fee, some offer magazines and discounts to writing related products.

Here are two that are specifically for romance writers-

Romance Writers of America www.rwa.org Annual membership fee is $95 plus $25 when you first join. You don't have to be published to apply for membership but certain groups within RWA won't be open to you if you're not. RWA is well established group that also has various chapters, mainly in each state of the US, but has special interest groups and an Internet chapter you can join (but you have to be a member of the RWA), fees to join the various chapters are additional. Many chapters also offer online workshops. RWA does offer an annual conference at various locations throughout the US.

Romantic Novelists Association, www.rna.co.uk Another well established group for the romance writer, both published and new. Fees are 50 pounds for writers based in the UK and EU and 57 pounds for the non EU based writer. Non-published members have to join the New Writer's Scheme which costs 120 pounds for the UK/EU based writer and 130 pounds for those not in the EU. Once accepted you need to submit a full length novel which will be read and appraised by published writers. If the reader feels your manuscript is ready they pass it along to an agent or publisher for further appraisal. Many writers have received contracts this through this scheme. Once accepted you then become a full member of the RNA. They have various local groups you can join, and also an online ROMNA group which is conducted through e-mail.

Looking for An Agent

If you want to look for an agent to represent you, check out this Web site first- www.aaronline.org

Reviewing

A great way to see what's being published and who's publishing what type of story is to become a reviewer. There are lots of sites on the Web and here are three to check out-

www.longandshortreviews.com Click on 'become a reviewer'
www.theromancereviews.com Click on 'become a reviewer'
www.coffeetimeromance.com

I know all owners of these sites so please feel free to use my name if you contact them.

Electronic Books

If you're interested in learning more about writing for the electronic market or electronic books in general one organization to check out is EPIC at www.epicorg.com Membership is $30 per year but you will need to have either a fiction or non-fiction book published (can be self-published) to be eligible for membership. They have an annual conference at various locations around the US and each year have the EPPIE awards for best electronic books in just about every category.

Finding a Critique Partner

If you're looking for some feedback for your work here are two places that I've found useful for finding a critique partner-

Harlequin Community- part of the Harlequin group which is useful for finding out about different lines and what's going on with Harlequin books and writers. And how I found my first critique partner www.community.harlequin.com

I found my second critique partner through a Yahoo group put together by The Wild Rose Press who published my first book. You don't have to be published by them as it's open to anyone it's called The Rose Trellis. Send an e-mail to Laura Kelly at laura@thewildrosepress.com and put Looking for A Critique Partner in the subject line and Laura will send you an invite to join the group and you can start posting messages.

Checking Out Publishers

One Web site that I've found is useful for getting feedback about publishers in www.duotape.com. Also, do a Google search on them too which should pull up reports of any problems writers have with a publisher.

Magazines to Check Out

If you want to check out some writing magazines that aren't romance specific but do offer lots of advice on many writing topics are Writer's Digest www.writersdigest.com and The Writer www.writermag.com and in the UK Writing Magazine www.writers-online.co.uk

One good resource for romance writers is Romantic Times www.rtbookreviews.com. Not a writing publication per se, but you'll good feel for what's being published and industry news. They also have a convention each April that offers a chance to meet other romance writers, editors, agents and take writing workshops.

Book Web Sites

And if you want to check out books online a couple of the big sites are www.allromanceebooks.com and www.fictionwise.com as well as www.amazon.com

About The Author

Susan Palmquist was born in London, England but now resides in the US. She's been writing since the late 80s and is now both a freelance writer, short story writer, blogger, and author. Her first romance novel, A Sterling Affair was published by The Wild Rose Press. Her work has also appeared in magazines and anthologies in both the US and UK. Under her pen name, she's bestselling author Vanessa Devereaux who is published with Cobblestone Press, Total E Bound and Evernight Publishing. As well as writing she's also a tutor for Writers' News Home Study Courses, and frequently teaches workshops through various chapters of the Romance Writers of America. Prior to her writing career she worked in PR and was a book publicist for three years. She's a member of RNA, EPIC and The Writer's Guild UK.

When she's not writing or teaching, she's either gardening, cooking, or riding her bike on the trails near her home.

For more information about Susan check out one of her Web sites, www.susanpalmquist.com, www.vanessadevereaux.com or www.thiswriterslife.com which she updates with her news of her workshops, writers tips, and industry interviews.

**COMPASS
BOOKS**

Compass Books focuses on practical and informative 'how-to' books for writers. Written by experienced authors who also have extensive experience of tutoring at the most popular creative writing workshops, the books offer an insight into the more specialised niches of the publishing game.